NO MATTER
WHICH WAY YOU LOOK,
THERE IS MORE TO SEE

The Collected Poems of

Kathie Giorgio

Finishing Line Press
Georgetown, Kentucky

NO MATTER
WHICH WAY YOU LOOK,
THERE IS MORE TO SEE

Publisher: Leah Maines

Editor: Christen Kincaid

Cover Art: Kathie Giorgio

Author Photo: Ron Wimmer

Cover Design: Elizabeth Maines McCleavy

Printed in the USA on acid-free paper.
Order online: www.finishinglinepress.com
            also available on amazon.com

Author inquiries and mail orders:
Finishing Line Press
P. O. Box 1626
Georgetown, Kentucky 40324
U. S. A.

Table of Contents

PART ONE:

Womanhood

PART TWO:

In Lust, In Love, In Grief, Intact

PART THREE:

The Writing Life

PART FOUR:

My Daughter, Olivia

Whirlwind Caught In Poetry

PART FIVE:

Cancer

PART SIX:

Nature, In & Out

PART SEVEN:

The End

For everyone.
Near, far
Here, there
Online, in my face
For everyone.

I'm an apostrophe
I'm just a symbol to remind you that there's more to see

—Imagine Dragons
"Whatever It Takes"

PART ONE:

Womanhood

PHOSPHENES

Prose poem

Phosphenes: Noun. The colors or the stars you see when you close your eyes.

Close. Squeeze.
The Yellow of summer after summer the sun painting you golden as you crawl in the sand as you walk as you swim as you stand ankle deep in the lake with your hands in your hair elbows cocked and hip out and you pose and Red fills you to burst in your heart in your veins flow with hope as you ask to go out with the boy six years older a man and your snarl is Red as your mother says no and you can't and you flare and the window is open Red heats down your breasts to your belly lights your way to the bar and the Redlit back alley and you give what you have who you are what you think that he wants and he's gone to a girl his own age a woman and Red clots and scalds and you cry in your pillow and your mother who said no braids your hair Purple stretches like puddles the good grades the class ring the gossip and the hand of a boy with Blue eyes who looks just at you and you dance the Blue starlight and you foxtrot for glory a diploma a job a wedding a layoff a baby a baby a fight there's no money a job then a house with a yard and a dog and a cat an affair his then yours a divorce and a cancer a song at a concert an online romance a marriage a late baby who stops breathing your arms are so empty but then Paris and Greece and soft Sunday mornings hot coffee cheese danish a grave with Red roses you say goodbye to your mother and Blue slows to Black the Black streaked with Silver the moon on your face a grandchild's gilded laughter a son's long embrace a gold clock encased in crystal and the night you sit by the ocean the water a silk whisper a warm blanket draped over your knees
Open. Open wide.
Brilliance.

TRIUMPH

I am 15 and you are 20
when you take me for a ride in your new car.
A TR-7.
The shape of things to come.
You are my cousin and we used to play
when I was 4 and you were 9
when I was 7 and you were 12.
But now you drive. You own a car.
The TR-7.
I've discovered cars.
I've discovered boys.
But I don't yet know what it means to be
a girl in a car with a boy.
The shape of things to come.

Ads siren-sing that sleek low car.
Pop-up lights that slice the night.
Tight curves, the leaping speed.
A garage shaped like a prism.
The shape of things to come.
That night, in that car, I look at you,
spill of black curls, new broad shoulders,
your boyhood face behind a beard, a mustache.
I watch the way you manhandle those gears.
Your hand like a fist.
I strap myself in, try to restrain these new curves
I don't know how to restrain
with your special order 5-point seatbelt.
You mash the gas and those batting-eye headlights
split the dark with the light of day and the engine
screams and so do we. Your arms flex straight and
my ass is pressed into the leather seat and
there we are. Launched.

Within the safety of a cousin, the net of memory
playing with Hot Wheels cars in the driveway gravel,
I become a girl in a car with a boy.

The shape of things to come.
I rip off my seatbelt and whoop.

ON THE SIDE OF THE ROAD

haiku

Woman walking black
flowing skirt leopard backpack
fashion plate of sass

APRIL FOOL IN FLORIDA

In front of me
through the window,
a dark-skinned woman
body flowing in a burnt
orange dress exposed
back exposed arms
kinked and coiled
hair held back
with a yellow silk scarf
works under the raised hood
of her white service van.
White towels sharp against
her skin, soon streaked black
with oil.

NO SECOND DATE

Love yourself, they said.
She tried.
Bought herself red roses.
Told herself she was lovely tonight.
Took herself to dinner.
Presented a bright shiny bracelet.
Romanced herself to bed.
Love yourself, they said.
Even then
she woke up alone.

DEEP

So we are larger
than our lives. What we hide,
we must bury deep

under our skin, breasts,
bones. We hide under our hearts.
Each beat a camouflage.

We are the circus
sideshow. Don't look to the high
wire. Look down at us

here. Deep dense skin our
costume and mask. What we hide,
we must bury deep.

IN THE THERAPIST'S OFFICE

I watch the girl on the red couch.
Rail thin body
rail thin dress
rail thin hair
rail thin stare straight ahead.
One leg scissored over the other
the dangling ankle vibrates
like a plucked string
rail thin flip-flop a successful
paddleball game against her sole.
Myself,
motionless
quiet
feet flat
lined-up knees
hands folded.
Before and After?
or After and Before?

HOW LATE WERE THE BOYS OUT?

prose poem

Everywhere She went, it seemed, She was the Mother. Even when She left Her child at home, Her child no longer, but a young woman of 13, even then, when She could let Her hair down, as they say, though Her hair was so short, there was no let-down, She was the Mother:

To the child
wandering through the restaurant, no parents in sight, wandering with arms out like the blind. The Mother was up off Her seat, Her arms out too, ready to catch, to comfort, a smile already on Her face that any child would recognize as safe. But before She got there, a woman, fast-fast, scooped the child up and away. Gave Her a look. And then the Mother returned to Her meal. Her own daughter was at home. Watching television, most likely.

To the teen
on a street corner in spring and the rain when it was still cold enough to turn fast to snow and he was soaked and there was no jacket. His hands were shoved like pool table balls in his pockets and the Mother pictured them both as the eight-ball, black and curved with a spot of violent white and a black mobius strip, around and around endlessly. She pulled over, rolled down Her window, offered a ride and Her face that any child would recognize as safe, but then there was a shout and more teens mobiused around and around the corner and the boy shrugged ice raindrops and he left. The Mother wondered then if Her daughter took a coat that morning. And She continued on Her way to work.

Even to the old woman
sitting outside of a rest home, resting since that's what she was there to do, and she had on a duster, a blue flowered duster and it hung between her knees and ankles like a grand curtain coming down. Down on a show that ran overtime, that ran for a lifetime, that made records in the annals of theater. Her hair was done in tight curls to her head silver and white and some strands of gray and the Mother thought of an ancient flower garden. The old woman sat there alone, her hands on a cane, an attempt at humor from someone, it was striped like the candy, but instead of holiday, instead of ho ho ho, it looked ridiculous on this woman who had once been a girl, who maybe wore a pink bikini, who the Mother pictured dreaming of a lifetime on stage, and maybe

achieved it. Even to the old, the Mother went up, sat down for a while, offered words on the day and the News and the weather, a story or two of Her own mother, gone now, whose hair had been red and ringleted to her waist until she died. The Mother described it spread out on the coffin pillow, like a shawl thrown back to the wind, but then She stopped because this woman was old and no mother should speak of death when that curtain was sweeping the floor. The Mother looked at her with a face that any child would recognize as safe and the woman nodded without saying a word, hung her chin on a mobius of red-pink-white-red-pink-white and fell asleep. The Mother's daughter, at home, TV.

And then a business trip
tucked in the middle of spring break, a trip to the South Carolina shore. Where she didn't have to be the Mother, not on the fourteenth floor, looking over the ocean, the female ocean, the Mother of all on Earth. She felt that, looking out, and thought that maybe, just maybe, She could give up this responsibility for a while. The ocean was here, to take care of things, and Her daughter was at home, safe with her father, and the Mother was here and alone.

But so were the college boys
next door and they hooted and hollered and they spat from their fourteenth floor to see what they could hit. The Mother stood unseen (as mothers do) on the balcony beside them, a solid wall between them, and She watched their saliva take wing and splatter on the sand. On a golf cart. On the top of a flying blue Frisbee. Bingo! And on a girl in a pink bikini, like the bikini Her daughter wore and the Mother had to look away when she did. The boys hooted and hollered until late at night when she wanted to urge them to bed, pull the blankets up, tell them the ocean (and their spit and the girls) would stillbe there in the morning. But then their voices rang in the hall and they left. Left at eleven o'clock at night. She waited up until one and then fell asleep on the unmade bed, Her head toward the television, which Her daughter was likely watching, though it was an hour earlier at home. Only midnight.

The Mother woke up in the quiet.
She opened the balcony door and stepped out and the ocean said good morning and asked how she slept. There were no boys next door. There was no spit, no hoots. From down below, there were the shouts of families and their children. Their daughters danced in the waves and She imagined her daughter there, in

her pink bikini, but on a flat chest, on round baby hips, the squeal a song in the waves. The Mother's hand out, one hand always out, and her baby always ready to grasp it. Even as she pulled away, snapping their joints taut, leaning out over the water.

Even when she wouldn't come to the phone?

With her mother so far away?

As the morning sounds built, the balcony door beside her slammed shut. She rested her cheek on the wall. She pictured blankets tucked to chins. She pictured her own empty hands.

How late were the boys out?

Time to phone home.

CONSIDER YOURSELF LUCKY

When she didn't like her bologna sandwich,
her mother talked about starving children in Africa.

When her eyes were blackened by the big kids at school,
her mother talked about the tribes in Sudan.

When she wasn't asked to the homecoming dance,
her mother talked about the lepers in Molokai.

When she graduated from college with a 4.0,
her mother talked about teenagers at Harvard.

When her husband was mad and broke two of her ribs,
her mother talked about burkas in Palestine.

When she gave birth to a beautiful girl,
her mother talked about a manger in Bethlehem.

When her husband was found in the arms of another,
her mother talked about polygamy in Utah.

When she was laid off and her house was foreclosed,
her mother talked about tornadoes in the south.

When she lost her mother, she gave a thoughtful eulogy
About all who were earthquaked in Japan.

And when her beautiful girl said that she didn't like bologna,
She said children were starving in Africa.

WONDER BREAD

(12 Ways)

1. summer sack lunches on bike handlebars
2. peanut butter and milk and after-school specials
3. bologna trade-ins for ham with orange cheese
4. toast after a bout with the flu
5. dark nightmare chaser, chastened with honey
6. shared shreds for the ducks on the creek
7. quartered and sugar-buttered for sleepover crumbs
8. slather-jelly on cartoon Saturdays
9. stripped crusts twirl brown on catfish hooks
10. big brat brother-bounced edible spitballs
11. redgreenyellow packageballoons on gray winter mornings
12. forty years later, eating twiggy bread, wishing for
    wonder once more.

MENU

On my plate for Monday lunch:
A piece and a half of Sunday supreme pizza
A fried golden chicken wing from Saturday dinner
Coleslaw from Friday Night Fish Fry
A bite of Sunday morning doughnut.

Surrounded by cubicle gray
Instructions and screens
And chore after chore after chore
I taste the weekend again
And day-after-daydream of what's
To come.

CRAVE

getting older
old
you find yourself
craving fruit
(clementines, peaches, pears, pears, pears!)
vegetables
(zucchini, green beans, cucumbers)
instead of the meat
of your youth
(ribs, porterhouse, ¼ pound burger, rare)
eating safe now
instead of then
but craving then
again

56

I wear a new Red shirt
My toenails are Red too
I walk the Blue ocean
and count the waves
to fifty-five.
Then more roll in. And more.
Tumble like Time.
But I stop counting.

THE DRIVE FROM PHOENIX TO SEDONA

Drove through Earth's old age today,
arthritic vein and cancer gore,
red bruise and ashy scar.
Drove straight through to life's desire,
to stand
then stand some more.

THE DRIVE FROM SEDONA
TO THE GRAND CANYON

Drove through Earth's guts today
colon roads
varicose trees
flowing arteries through rock hard muscle.

And then the Grand Canyon.
The open chest of the World.

Layers of red tissue and green mass
pink muscle
white bone fragments and hard work
striated stress and heavy love
pulled aside to expose
Earth's heart.

Laid open for
the Healer's hand.

Elbow-deep in ancient medicine
the Healer touched the Earth
and wasn't too busy to turn
and touch me too.

RENTAL CAR

My rental car has no key.
It starts with a push button.
Like George Jetson. Like space.
Like Hal 9000.
But it can't make coffee.
The future isn't bright.
Yet.

BUMPS IN THE ROAD

Yep. I think it's time.
Missed This.
Hot That.
Slow descent into the Desert of Dry.
Time to Wax Poetical.
Moon Tides!
Ocean Waves!
Girl, Maiden, Crone!
Aw, crap.
I have one leg so far in the grave
the other is kneeling by my Headstone.
Yikes.
I'd rather Wax Poetical.
Wisdom and Knowledge pour out like the Hot Sweat of Mother Earth!
Ancient Voices whisper to me and
welcome me to the Sacred Circle!
…
Oh, fuck it. I'm old.

CRONEMAIDEN

I am from Wisconsin.
But I find myself in Maine.
Beaches that aren't beaches
at all but resting places
graveyards
for ocean-smoothed and discarded
Rocks.
The Atlantic breathes salt water
my bare feet can't touch because
of the rock's bite.
Earth's skeleton lost teeth.
Sitting on a bench stripped
of color by the thick-grained air
I am young next to the
Earth's still maiden ocean.
Still maiden despite years of
Forever.
But the knock of my hip bones
my own skeleton
reminds me that while
the maiden has Forever
this crone doesn't.

HEAT

Lady Ocean and Mother Moon
join hands, enclose a circle
and waves of salt and silvershine
cool this new yet ancient heat
simmering in me.

Embers crackle my bones, pop
ashes when I stretch my fingers
roll my shoulders bend my legs.

Melding my experiences and
words and colors and meanings
into an unfamiliar, echoed
wisdom.

Past and present melt and mix
into Crone.

SATAN

haiku

The past is always
Here and now and up ahead.
Get thee behind me.

WOMAN OF AN AGE

A Poetic Proclamation

"You can come, but it's probably not your thing," my young friend said to me.
Not my thing.
Bare bodies on a beach, pounding balls, roasting hot dogs, staring into fires and
singing.
Not my thing.
Bare bodies pumping, humping the motions of The Act, exposed stabs of stimulation.
Not my thing.

HA!

I am a Woman of An Age.
Knowledge soaks my skin and
Experience whorls my fingertips.
Words thrill off my tongue to curve in the ears of men
who thrill even more when my Consonants touch their chests
and Verbs writhe against the roofs of their mouths.
My Vowels activate erogenous zones they don't even know they have.

I know everything there is to know and
I am Satisfaction-soaked to my core.
There is no frantic in my thighs
but the patient thrum of knowing what will come,
that it will be good, that there is always more, and that
a held breath can be as intense as a scream.

Hours of experience are so much deeper than the minutes of youth.
Hunger saturates me, but I know I will be fed and that I will grow hungry again.
There is no end. I see God and my Heaven is here. Certain Death is to be repeated.

I am durable.

An erotic education has eased my hips, my thighs, my wrists and my jaw,
once stiff with the fear of performance, of low grades, of another's dissatisfaction.
Now I undulate undercover in a mix of silk and salt as
my joints all unhinge for multiple exchanges of joy.

Everything about me is high grade.
Everything about me is satisfaction guaranteed.
I bask in the heat of an ageless sun and what radiates from me
melts the most hardened of men.

Not my thing, my young friend said.
Not my thing.
As if my thing is bare bodies low on the learning curve.
The translucent facsimiles of the future. The stabs of stimulation
And hurried inexperience.
In years to come, he will know the luxury of age
And patience and all 20,000 leagues of lust.
He will remember me
And wonder just what he missed.

A Woman of an Age.

SHE DID WHAT SHE COULD

She stands draped
in shreds of afterdeath
and reads her stone:
She did what she could.
She looks at her wrist
Ephemeral now
And missing the bracelet
She always wore.
It said:
She believed she could, so she did.
The bracelet is underground.
And she wonders what happened.

PART TWO:

In Lust, In Love, In Grief, Intact

TANNING

Sweet sin of sun
rosying my skin
Heat hovers like a
favored lover.
My joints ease with desire.

Oh, let me be evil.
I don't care about Hell.
Layer me in the heat
Of the Devil himself.

VELVET VOICE

haiku

When you speak velvet,
women sweat out estrogen
puddles you suck dry.

BODY KNOWLEDGE

We coerce in body knowledge
and twist into a verb
Raw slipstream motion and
Tangy salt of sex exertion
creates connections of stroke and slide
Tongues to thighs, lips to lobes, fingers
and palm and thumb
Our crooned expletives sweat lyrical
Take me
Use me
Fuck me
Touch here and here,
and oh please there
We blur into Hurts-So-
Good immersion
and lose our boundaries
to bliss.

FEAST

I am warm and waking-drowsy
when you come into our bed
bearing coffee and cheese danish
and baring yourself too.

Our sheets are a tablecloth and you spread
naked before me, an audacious feast.
You know the reality of my appetite
and I've memorized the menu.
I sip and swallow and savor.

Your ribcage, slender and smooth, forms
a platter beneath my fingers and I swoop
across your skin like fine china.

Bowl stomach reminds me of those coin
collectors in the mall where the pennies
race each other in swirls before dropping
down an endless belly button. My fingers
spiral and you gasp.

My eyes' caress brings you erect and I raise
your wares to the table to fill my mouth
with course after course. Tongue the tines,
the bowl, the knife's serrated edge.
Your spices are as packed and flavorful as
any salt and pepper. Ready to sprinkle
liberally to my taste.

The coffee is gone and the danish set aside as I
open myself for the main course, for filling myself
overfull, overstuffed. I am a glutton. More and more
and more. Please.
Your feasty body appeals to my gourmet tastes
in all seasons, all holidays, all days and nights
and all the minutes in between.

Summer's straddle and sweat.
Fall's tumble and burn.
Winter's face to face heated embrace and
Spring's rebirth with you bursting between my legs.

Oh, you are delicious.

When you kiss me sated, your lips are as soft as
any linen napkin. Your tongue is a breath-mint
in my mouth.

Time for dessert.

CAUGHT

villanelle

Oh, babe, you tempt me again.
My body's wick flickers alight.
Our fate was lost, and now regained.

Please surge this spark into a flame,
a hidden pyre engulfing our night.
Oh, babe, you tempt me again.

Without this heat, no soul remains.
Cold and stiff, I plead for Fire!
Our fate was lost, and now regained.

My skin wants to sear onto your frame;
please strike the match and free the burn.
Oh, babe, you tempt me again.

The black of abstinence leaves my heart in pain.
White passion simmers beneath the calm.
Our fate was lost, and now regained.

Temptation inflamed when Eros trains
his sight on the likes of us.
Our fate was lost, and now regained.
Oh, babe, you tempt me again.

YOU ARE

haiku

Under my skin, in
side my heart and I'm in heat
and in love with you.

RAPTURE

On the day of the Rapture,
(either the world's end, with blood
skies and ruptured clouds and lightning
shearing the moon…
Or the moment when my body rises
off the bed, pulses nature's drumbeat and heat
shimmers from me in ancient rivers…),
On the day of the Rapture
(either/or),
I want to be with you.

PUZZLE

haiku

He says he doesn't
like people much. I wonder
how he can love me.

DOMINOES

I love you more than I've ever loved anyone,
he says, and then he looks over her shoulder,
winks at another woman and walks away.
She waits in his echo for months,
joining others who stand in a long line
facing west.
And then like dominoes,
they fall.

POOF

haiku

So what happens when
those you love become strangers?
Your heart disappears.

ALONE

haiku

Seems on days when things
are normal, you're more missing
and missed than ever.

BY AND BY

When she takes off her wedding ring,
lays it gently on their kitchen table
the circle is still unbroken.
But she is shattered.

GRIEF MAKES A MEAL

Grief makes a meal, munches memories and heartbeats
places his lips on her bloodline, sucks the vein like spaghetti
just like in that movie, but in this case, there is no lady.
There is only a tramp.

Grief moves his mouth around her, makes splinters of her bones
remembers the way he mounted them before, smashes them now.
His tongue hovers in all the special places, but the taste Grief tastes now
isn't pleasure but possession.

He leaves her skin like shellac, a shell that is translucent with nothing
no one
inside.

IN TRAINING

haiku

Kubler-Ross was wrong.
Only Five Steps? Many more.
Marathon through hell.

LEFT BEHIND

haiku

Grief for one who breathes!
The sight, the sound, rips adhesive.
Bandage again. Again.

TODAY'S REFUGE

prose poem

I used to believe the gods feigned blindness to the folly of love,
deafness to our prayers and pleadings. Now I know that the old gods are dead
(Anteros, Luamerava, Qadesh). Gone the way of Leda and the Swan. We love to
die, and we die to love on, some say, as animals and beasts – a snake of fantasy
in the pulse machine that breathed the maker's words into passion. Today my
one refuge is this body I cling to, a shell in need of sustenance – poetry and
warm salt waters to tame its unruly spirit. One day this prison will dissolve and
my soul, like the heat of sex, shall rise above the bed of the earth, and follow the
path of ancestors to the heavens and linger there among the new gods (in the
name of the father, the son, and the holy ghost) to contemplate the uncertainty
of who we were and whom we loved.

INTIMACY

After a lifetime
of swapping spit
and sharing germs
stealing bases
and running home
feeling up
and going down
wet kissing
and dry humping
getting laid
and getting screwed
coming
and going,

it's so nice
to just hold hands.

AFTERGLOW

haiku

The sun on my bed
drifts me to warm nights of play
under a red quilt.

PART THREE:

The Writing Life

EASING THE WORDS

When the warm stone is pressed into my palm
My fingers close around it and every knuckle cracks
Amazing the muscles used in writing
Shoulders hunched at the keyboard
Hands striking, restriking, remarking, refining
Words on a screen for a page someplace else.
For someone else.

Warm stones eased on shoulders, pressed down to a stretch
Tendons and joints release storylines
Grow supple for new plots and turns.

Warm stones on the ears, pull the lobes, press behind
Empty the voices and the voices and the voices
Protagonists
Antagonists
And the secondaries, especially that one, who
Strides to the front of the brain and insists he's not
Secondary and lopes off into a story of his own, before the
Last is finished and so suddenly, there are two storypaths
Twisting in my brain, two trains of thought, two begging to be
Done and up front and alone.
Stones on the ears, tugs and stretches
Make room for the new voices just waiting.

Warm stones on the temples and then placed on the eyes and
Turn to salty river rocks as tears stream down my cheeks.
There is no story, after all, without conflict.

TEACHING MEMOIR

Knee-deep dirt
outside of bedrooms
some pink some blue
double bed or twin
dorm or hotel or upstairs,
second door on the right.

Carted in squeaky wheel
barrows and laid, wormy
on the classroom table
I shovel it out the back door
add it to compost pile
started with my own.

When the table is clean
replaced with black words on
the whitest of paper, unmarred,
under control
Then shoulders straighten and smiles
burst and eyes are cleared with years
of shit-filled hallways behind them.

I stand by the compost pile,
pound after pound of pain,
fermenting tall and wide
And I wonder when it will be full and when
I can set fire to it all.

COMMA

Through history and lives,
and loves,
in letters, telegrams, postcards,
emails, tweets and texts,
a proper comma keeps thousands
from speaking the truth.
From letting hearts spell
their full request:
Love, Me (we signed)
Love Me (we said)

WHEN OTHERS KILL YOUR DARLINGS

Through my window, I watch the whales
rise and spout ebb and flow
and they watch me throw my words
shape them like sand castles
defenseless to the tide.

At the end of the day, I wish my words
on paper instead. Not blinking on a screen.
Blinking like the blind.
On paper, I could bring them to the edge of the sea
shred them
fly them like confetti kites on the waves
to the great jaws of the whales

let my words be swallowed like Jonah
inhabit the safe caverns of their ribs
float on the salt water in their bellies
find a home beneath the biggest
of hearts.

RETURN FROM RETREAT

And just like that, I step back
into my life.
Leaving behind the halls of daydreams
the glances out others' eyes
the grab and suck of other lives
a self-stuck drip of emotion.

In the land of dreamy dreams
there are tales of burning love
and a fear of flying over the Hotel
New Hampshire, leaving behind
the places I've been.
So raise high the roofbeam, carpenters,
as I lay dying in leaves of grass.

And for me, there is a house
of a hundred thousand clocks
moving forward on heart and soul and blood,
where the rhythm just won't be stopped.

There are Fat Girls walking sidewalks
one leg buried in the grave
all voices turned to the moon
and their hearts so full to bursting.

There's a girl with secret tattoos
and a woman in memory's garden
and now a rose, alone at night,
circled with smoke and semen.

I've been in the good company of others
and the close company of my own
these very last two weeks.
And just like that, I step back
into my life. But I bear all of their
secrets. And my own.

PART FOUR:

My Daughter, Olivia,
Whirlwind Caught In Poetry

THE DRIVE HOME AFTER SCHOOL LOCKDOWN

(there she is!)
Mama, did you about have a heart attack?
(yes)
I'm okay.
Mia'n'me went into tech ed
and we hid under a table.
We chit-chatted.
(about?)
Sonic the Hedgehog.
He's fast, you know. And blue.
And about fashion. We
want to wear capris and tank tops.
Don't you think it's warm enough?
(chilled)
Brianna was under the table next door.
She was alone.
She knocked on our table. Lots of times.
I think she was scared. I don't
like Brianna. But I let her knock.
It was okay.
But I still don't like her.
We got to miss math!
(3 hours. 180 minutes. 10,800 seconds.)
Didn't get to miss science though.
When they said clear, we crawled
out from under the table.
Like amoebas.
Like in lakes. Did you know you could die
if you swallow an amoeba in a lake?
I hope we get to miss math
again tomorrow.
(17 hours until I have to leave you here again)
Mama?
I don't want to ever
(home safe home safe home)
swim in a lake again.

CURVES

My girl starts to curve.
Out and in with gentle
undulations.
In her swimsuit, there are dips and
flares of pink and skin in
what were once innocent
cut-outs.
She is a beautiful child.
She will be a beautiful woman.

At home, diet drugs spark
across the tv screen,
she asks to buy them.
"I'm too fat, Mama," she says.
"Ninety pounds!" She pats the tummy
that used to be round, but now bowls in.
I look at her and think of swooping.

I am thrown back to another mother
another daughter.
Nude in front of a mirror, forced to stare
at new curves.
I thought ugly curves.
I swooped my fingers over ribs
and clasped my knuckles over barnacles.
Fat bulged through my fingers.
Even as I felt bone.
"Look how huge!" she yelled.
"Just look at that!"
Ninety pounds.
And twelve years old.

"Mama?" my daughter says. "Mama."
She stands behind me, circles her arms
around my neck, kisses the top of my head.
I poke my eyes up at her and think, Oh, look.
Just look at her.

We stand in front of my mirror and I
tell her about the glory I see.
All her glory.
Oh, just look.
And she sees the glory in me.

She is a beautiful child.
She will be a beautiful woman.

DEFIANCE RELFECTED

a running haiku

The hot water tank
dumps its load for you as your
preteen daughter sits

in her sullen room,
wrapped in a too-small bathrobe
with peace signs and snags.

It is nine o'clock.
Time for her steamy shower
lost in mist and dream.

Your skin pinks and swells.
Bubbles fill silver and paths
of four pregnancies

and late nights waiting.
Colic. Nightmares. Love.
Dates in springtime's heat.

Three before her took
showers in the spring and heat
sent them far from home.

She is your last and
she is ready to combust.
You soak in the tub.

Let her sit in her
new juices, let her stew in her
heat. You make her wait.

DAUGHTER WASHING CAR

My daughter stands tiptoe in the driveway.
She wears a star-splashed bikini.
She is washing her car.
A VW Beetle with pink eyelashes she's named Starlight Lashes.
The pink plastic lashes and the name are all I have left of my little girl.
I feel 500 years old.
And I want a bikini.

PART FIVE:

Cancer

(I have only honored breast cancer with two poems.
I doubt there will be any more. I prefer to honor survivorship.)

WHAT DOESN'T KILL YOU

Every day
as I lay naked under
the external beam
radiation machine,
my legs bound
my arms over my head
in full arrest,

it tears me apart
breaks me down
from the inside out.

it tells me
this is for my own good
it tells me
this is what I deserve.

So did he.

And every day
I hear the truth of it
Now
I hear the lie of it
then
but I know that
just like before
just like then
I will come out of this
stronger
and alive.

SEX AFTER BREAST CANCER

You are your rebuke
repeating a mantra,
Be happy to be alive.
A part of you died
while the rest ran for safety
as the leper was excised
from your body.
Be happy. I'm alive.

You switch the refrain
from time to time
I'm lucky I'm lucky So lucky
you still have two breasts.
But in front of the mirror,
one plus one does not equal two.
You have one whole breast
and one not so whole.
Two-thirds. Maybe.

That sad breast
collapsed on one side
nipple pointing to the right
like a tattletale finger
areola no longer a pearl-pink halo
but a white ghost of what was
That sad breast
You cradle it with one hand
and hide it from your sight
glance over your shoulder
at the empty bed behind you.
Be happy. I'm so lucky.

You remember that pose
that pose
I am happy to be alive!
Those moments
I got lucky I'm lucky So lucky!

Arms flung over your head
Bare
Naked
On display
A mating dance
A ritual
Your breasts two whole magnets
for your lover's
Lovers'
mouth tongue teeth hands
Love
Admiration

But now
And now
Well…now
you know if he or he or he or even He
was here
you'd cross your arms over your breasts
one hand cradling
hiding
and you'd run from the room.
You rebuke.
Be happy.

Cradling your breast
your sad breast
two-thirds here one-third excised
you wonder if the only touch
you will ever feel now
is your own.
Hiding.
Be happy to be alive.
I'm lucky. I'm lucky. So lucky.

PART SIX:

Nature
In & Out

FIRST MOMENT OF SPRING

haiku

New birdsong splits snow
into crystal vases of
crocus-tulipped spring!

THIS MORNING BY THE SEA

This morning I walk by the crazy-ass sea
that is too cold to swim in
And I wear jeans and a long-sleeved shirt
a hooded sweatshirt, sneakers
in July.
Not capris and a t-shirt and sandals
that I wore in Myrtle Beach
in March.
I think of brown-skinned children
in neon swimsuits in the surf and sun and sand
And I watch children here, in neon swimsuits
jumping in the water
skin turning sea-blue
while their parents wear sweatshirts and jeans and sneakers
and shake their heads because you just can't keep children
from the water.
And I wait for the shriek of a child stung by
a jellyfish
and wonder if the mother will sweep the child up
run for the house the car the doctor
or remember that episode of Friends
and then squat down to pee on her child's foot
and the child's scream will be more about a mother's love
than the sting.
And I wonder why I feel so at home here
by this crazy-ass sea too cold to swim in
where my nose runs like March in Wisconsin
in Oregon's July.
I dream of the hot mug of coffee I will suck down
as soon as I hurry to my makeshift desk in the cottage
overlooking the crazy-ass sea.
When I am walking by the sea, I dream of my desk,
and when I am at my desk, I dream of walking by the sea.
And at night in my bed, I hear the sea and see the dark and
look at my desk and fight sleep because there's so much
I want to do.
I am never fully at peace, always clamoring.

Like this crazy-ass sea too cold to swim in
reaching for the beach, then pulling back to the deep.
Clawing for the beach, then surging back to the deep.
…Oh…
At home, I sit by my own space heater
while the furnace blows
while the air conditioning blows
when the windows are open to allow spring
to chase away winter.
My bones are always Minnesota March cold
even though I haven't lived in northern Minnesota
for forty-four years.
I am as cold as this crazy-ass sea that is too cold to swim in.
…Oh…
This crazy-ass sea and I are cold-blooded sisters.
But I don't believe I am too cold to swim in.

THE OCEAN

haiku

heaves Death out of reach,
sobs in shuddering waves, rubs
salt in hopeless wounds

LIMITS TO FREEDOM

In my mind's eye
the river loops
swinging down and around
and back again in a never
ending highway of swirling water.
Down to the south,
up to the north,
rolling east and west,
circumnavigating its journey.
In reality, the river starts here
and ends there.
The water flows only one way.
I like my mind's river better.

IN THE PRISON ART GALLERY AND GIFT SHOP

prose poem

Smooth glossed, shapely curves. Ducks with secret carved insides. Gnomes. Boats. Paintings thick with rolling acrylic and plastic shine. The Ocean. The Lighthouse. The Forest. The Cabin. Pinks, greens, textured dipping blues meant to show the sea the painter can't see anymore from behind thick bars and concrete walls. Everything in this gallery is made by shackled hands. By men who did something so bad as to become "incarcerated." Harsh word. Like lacerated. Those hands touched these things that I touch now. Sanded the slivers and splinters and broken grain, maybe embedding one or two in a callous thumb or a cruel palm. Painted the colors, smoothed the clear and glistening stain. The stain. I select the duck with the secret insides. Run a finger over its bill. Heft it. Pull out the head to see the hollowed gullet. Treasure keeper. Secret chamber. Empty. Over and over, I run my fingers inside it. And out.

There is no heart at all.

FOX RIVERWALK, DUSK

haiku

Riverslow; soft, dark.
Fireflies light the synapses.
Frogsong thrums the pulse.

MAINE COAST EVENING

haiku

In the blue evening
a dog's bark punctures the sea
spills salt on the wind.

CRICKETS

At night, the canned crickets
chirp inside my sound machine
on my bedside table.
And I sleep to their rhythm.
Dream to the steady of it.
In sunlight, on my walk, the
crickets chirp in broken sounds in
the green and yellow on my
right and my left.
Unsteady. Surprise.
And I don't feel sleepy at all.

BOOM (!)

haiku

Thunderstorm at night
exclamation point for a
day that went too long.

HARVEST MOON

haiku

The moon at half mast
glows silver dreams and gold truths
as sighs twirl the earth

FAITH

I turn the lamp off by my bedside
and the dark closes immediate
complete.
But I know in seconds I
will see again.
Without any light at all.

PART SEVEN:

The End

TAKE MY LEAVE

When I go
I'll have a massage first
Warm stones against a taxed body
Warm stones against a taxed mind
And so connect with the earth which
will gentle me in
cloak me in silence and
stillness and soft, soft home.

When I take my leave
I will be serene
not scared
at peace
Let go

As the warm stones melt
my body into lax and loose
muscles and soft, soft skin,
my mind will melt too
and in death will come
Freedom.

THE END

ACKNOWLEDGEMENTS

The following poems have appeared previously in the listed magazines and anthologies:

Al-Khernia Poetica: "Sex After Breast Cancer"
Awakenings Review: "Yellow"
Awakenings Review: "In The Therapist's Office"
Awakenings Review: "Grief Makes A Meal"
Awakenings Review: "In The Prison Art Gallery And Gift Shop"
Brain, Child: "Defiance Reflected"
Chuffed Buff Books, Journey to Crone anthology: "Bumps In The Road"
Chuffed Buff Books, "Maine Coast Evening"
Cliterature: "Feast"
Dying Dahlia Review: "Crave"
Earth's Daughters: "What Doesn't Kill You"
Edify Fiction: "Rapture"
Fearless Books Fearless Poetry Series, Touching: Poems of Love, Longing, and Desire anthology: "Intimacy", published originally as "In Retrospect"
Finishing Line Press: "Dominoes", from the chapbook, When You Finally Said No
Gyroscope Review: "Woman Of An Age"
The Light Journal: "Comma"
The Main Street Rag: "Phosphenes"
The Main Street Rag: "Triumph"
The Main Street Rag Publishing Company, Bars & Burgers anthology: "Menu"
Minerva Rising: "Deep"
Poetic Diversity: "Crickets"
Poetic Diversity: "Faith"
Poetic Diversity: "Rental Car"
Voice of Eve: "Daughter Washing Car"
Voice of Eve: "Afterglow"
Voice of Eve: "On The Side Of The Road"
Wisconsin Poets 2012 Calendar: "Tanning"
Wisconsin Poets 2013 Calendar: "Wonder Bread: 12 Ways"
Wisconsin Poets 2018 Calendar: "April Fool In Florida"
Wisconsin Poets 2020 Calendar: "The Drive From Sedona To The Grand Canyon"

The poem, "Curves", was performed by professional actresses at the Normal In Schools Inside Out Annual Gala, held at the Turner Ballroom in Milwaukee, Wisconsin.

The poem, "Sex After Breast Cancer", was nominated for Sundress Publication's 2019 Best of the Net anthology.

The poem, "Crickets", was nominated for a Pushcart Prize.

The poem, "Harvest Moon", was included in the Poetry Leaves exhibition in Waterford, MI, and included in the 2020 Poetry Leaves anthology.

KATHIE GIORGIO is the critically acclaimed author of five novels, *The Home For Wayward Clocks* (2011), *Learning To Tell (A Life)Time* (2013), *Rise From The River* (2015), *In Grace's Time* (2017), and *If You Tame Me* (2019), two story collections, *Enlarged Hearts* (2012) and *Oddities & Endings; The Collected Stories Of Kathie Giorgio* (2016), a collection of essays, *Today's Moment Of Happiness Despite The News; A Year Of Spontaneous Essays* (2018), and two poetry chapbooks, *True Light Falls In Many Forms* (2016) and *When You Finally Said No* (2019). *No Matter Which Way You Look, There Is More To See* is her first full-length poetry collection. Giorgio's short stories and poems have appeared in countless literary magazines and anthologies. Her short story, *Snapdragon*, was performed on stage for the Stories On Stage series at Su Teatro theatre in Boulder, Colorado. Her poem, *Harvest Moon*, appeared in the Poetry Leaves exhibit in May 2020 in Waterford, Michigan. She's been nominated in both fiction and poetry for the Pushcart Prize, the Write Well Award, the Million Writer Award, and for both fiction and poetry for the Best of the Net Anthology. Her novel *The Home For Wayward Clocks* won the 2011 Outstanding Achievement Award from the Wisconsin Library Association. Her novel *In Grace's Time* was runner-up in fiction in the 2017 Maxy Award and the second place winner of the 2017 Silver Pen Award For Literary Excellence. Her novel *If You Tame Me* won second place in the Women's Fiction category of the 2019 Pencraft Awards For Literary Excellence. Giorgio is the director/founder of AllWriters' Workplace & Workshop. She lives in Waukesha, Wisconsin, with her husband, mystery writer Michael Giorgio, her 19-year old daughter Olivia, who is writing her first novel, a neurotic dog named after Ursula LeGuin, a fat cat named Edgar Allen Paw, and a tiny cat named Muse.